SRA Specific Skill Series
for Reading

Identifying
Fact & Opinion

Sixth Edition

Columbus, OH

The **McGraw·Hill** Companies

SRAonline.com

 SRA

PURPOSE:

IDENTIFYING FACT AND OPINION is designed to help develop the important skill of understanding and recognizing the difference between facts and opinions. **IDENTIFYING FACT AND OPINION** requires students to analyze information and determine whether it can be researched and proved or if it is a feeling or belief.

FOR WHOM:

The skill **IDENTIFYING FACT AND OPINION** is developed through a series of books spanning ten levels (Picture, Preparatory, A, B, C, D, E, F, G, H). The Picture Level is for students who have not acquired a basic sight vocabulary. The Preparatory Level is for students who have a basic sight vocabulary but are not yet ready for the first-grade-level book. Books A through H are appropriate for students who can read on levels one through eight, respectively.

THE NEW EDITION:

The sixth edition of the *Specific Skill Series for Reading* maintains the quality and focus that has distinguished this program for more than 40 years. A key element central to the program's success has been the unique nature of the reading selections. Fiction and nonfiction pieces about current topics have been designed to stimulate the interest of students, motivating them to use the comprehension strategies they have learned to further their reading. To keep this important aspect of the program intact, a percentage of the reading selections has been replaced in order to ensure the continued relevance of the subject material.

In addition, a significant percentage of the artwork in the program has been replaced to give the books a contemporary look. The cover photographs are designed to appeal to readers of all ages.

SESSIONS:

Short practice sessions are the most effective. It is desirable to have a practice session every day or every other day, using a few units in each session.

SCORING:

Students should record their answers on the reproducible worksheets. The worksheets make scoring easier and provide uniform records of the students' work. Using worksheets also avoids consuming the exercise books.

It is important for students to know how well they are doing. For this reason, units should be scored as soon as they have been completed. Then a discussion can be held in which students justify their choices. (The *Language Activity Pages,* many of which are open-ended, do not lend themselves to an objective score; thus there are no answer keys for these pages.)

GENERAL INFORMATION ON *IDENTIFYING FACT AND OPINION:*

IDENTIFYING FACT AND OPINION varies in content. It contains fiction and nonfiction stories that will stretch the imagination, spark interest in new areas, promote admiration for outstanding achievements, and develop a sense of wonder about our world.

There is only one correct answer for each question. Students practice identifying facts and opinions they read in the story or see in the picture. **IDENTIFYING FACT AND OPINION** means recognizing which statements can be proven and which are feelings or beliefs.

SUGGESTED STEPS:

1. Students read the story. (In the Picture Level books, the students look at the pictures. In the Prep Level books, the students look at the pictures and listen to the stories.)

2. After completing the story, students answer the questions and choose the letter of the correct answer.

3. Students write the letters of the correct answers on the worksheets.

4. Students may refer back to the pictures and stories before choosing an answer.

RELATED MATERIALS:

Specific Skill Series Assessment Book provides the teacher with a pretest and a posttest for each skill at each grade level. These tests will help the teacher assess the students' performance in each of the nine comprehension skills.

A **fact** is something that is true. You can check a fact to make sure that it is true. These are facts:

> Oranges grow on trees.
> Horses have four legs.

An **opinion** is a feeling, idea, or belief. You cannot check to see if an opinion is true or false. These are opinions:

> Fall is the most beautiful time of the year.
> Snowboarding is really exciting.

You can look for facts and opinions as you read. You can look for facts in pictures too. A picture of a girl throwing a ball for a dog contains these facts:

> There is one girl and one dog in the picture.
> The girl and the dog are playing with a ball.

There are 50 units in this book. For each unit, think about the pictures carefully. Then answer the questions about the pictures.

Tara made the sign. Mason made the juice. It is a hot day. They sold five cups of juice.

Which sentence tells a fact?

(A) Tara and Mason share the work.

(B) It is too hot to sell juice.

Carlos helps Aunt Marissa shop. He gets the jar for her. She buys the crackers for him.

Which sentence tells an opinion?

    (A) Aunt Marissa cannot reach all the food.

    (B) Crackers are the best snack.

Jason is weeding the garden. Amy gives weeds to the goats. The goats eat the weeds.

Which sentence tells an opinion?

    (A) Weeds grow in the garden.

    (B) No one likes weeds.

Rosa and Luis like dogs. They take five dogs for a walk. Mrs. Grey gives them a dollar to walk her dogs.

Which sentence tells a fact?

(**A**) It is fun to walk dogs.

(**B**) Dogs and cats have four legs.

Sara paints one wall. Sara's mom paints the next wall. The work goes fast.

Which sentence tells a fact?

(A) A paintbrush or roller is used to paint.

(B) The room will look nice.

Mom and Ty made a big pile. They worked hard. Now it is time to play. They jump into the leaves.

Which sentence tells an opinion?

(A) Some trees lose their leaves in the fall.

(B) The leaves smell good.

Jan reads to Grandpa. Jake brings a snack.
They have a nice visit.

Which sentence tells a fact?

(**A**) Grandpa eats apples.

(**B**) The apples are great.

Lee plays with Baby Kim. He shows her a new game. They play peek-a-boo. Kim learns fast.

Which sentence tells an opinion?

(**A**) Kim is a smart baby.

(**B**) Lee and Kim are brother and sister.

Mom and Kia go to a yard sale. Mom buys a mat. Kia buys a book and a soccer ball.

Which sentence tells a fact?

(A) Yard sales are fun.

14

(B) Kia and Mom find things they want.

José and Papa go out for lunch. José wants to try a new food. He orders an egg roll.

Which sentence tells an opinion?

(A) Egg rolls taste good.

(B) José has never eaten an egg roll.

The piano teacher is proud of Zoe. She learned to play the song well. Rex, the dog, likes the song too.

Which sentence tells an opinion?

(A) Zoe played a song on the piano.

(B) Piano music sounds pretty.

Steve likes to take pictures. He walks out to the end of the dock. He takes a picture of the sunset.

Which sentence tells a fact?

(A) Steve takes good pictures.

(B) Steve knows how to use a camera.

Write the information below on the board or chart paper.

Jobs

Weed the garden	$2.00
Walk the dogs	$1.00
Dust the shelves	$0.75
Fold the towels	$0.50

A. Exercising Your Skill

Talk about the list of jobs on the board. Tell the students you are going to read a sentence and they are to decide which job it matches from the list. Discuss their answers.

1. If you sneeze often, these jobs will be too hard.
2. This job pays the most money.
3. This is the easiest job.
4. These two jobs are done outside.

B. Expanding Your Skill

With the class make a list of the jobs students do. Write the list on the board. Choose a job, and pretend that you are doing that job. Tell one fact about that job. Tell your opinion about the job. See if the class can guess which job it is.

C. Exploring Language

Write the words below on the board.

three   big   hungry   many

Listen to the following story. Use the words on the board to fill in the blanks. Have a volunteer choose a word that makes sense in each sentence. Use each word once.

You have to make _____ little trips to do this job. If you have a lot of people in your family, your job is _____. You are usually _____ when you do this job. This job is often done _____ times a day.

What is this job?

D. Expressing Yourself

Do one of these things.

1. Imagine that you own a store. Think about what you would sell in the store. Tell a partner the list of things that you would sell.

2. Think of a job you do at home. Draw a picture of yourself doing that job. Draw your face to show your opinion of the job.

Juan shows Max a book about dogs. Tessa reads about explorers. They like books.

Which sentence tells a fact?

   (A) Libraries have lots of books.

   (B) It is fun to read.

All kinds of pets came to the pet show. Each pet was the best at something. The dog was the loudest.

Which sentence tells an opinion?

(A) Each pet won a prize.

(B) Cats are the best pets.

Jen and Sam see many stars. Mom points out the Big Dipper in the sky.

Which sentence tells a fact?

    (A) It is fun to be out at night.

    (B) The Big Dipper is made of stars.

Sue kicks a goal. Reg misses the ball. The score is one to zero. Sue's team is in the lead.

Which sentence tells an opinion?

    (A) Soccer is the best sport.

    (B) If one team wins, the other loses.

Meg makes vegetable cars to eat. Grandma helps her cut. They think the cars are silly.

Which sentence tells an opinion?

(A) Most cars have four wheels.

(B) The cars taste great.

"Lewis and Clark traveled far," said Dad. "They met many people. They tried different kinds of food."

Which sentence tells a fact?

    (A) Lewis and Clark went on a journey.

    (B) This museum is interesting.

They pick lots of berries. Just a few are in the pails. The berries taste too good!

Which sentence tells a fact?

(A) Their lunch will not taste as good as the berries.

(B) The bear will not eat the berries.

Dad brings the flowers. Paul and Anji plant them. Now the front of the store looks nice.

Which sentence tells an opinion?

(A) They have many more flowers to plant.

(B) The flowers smell good.

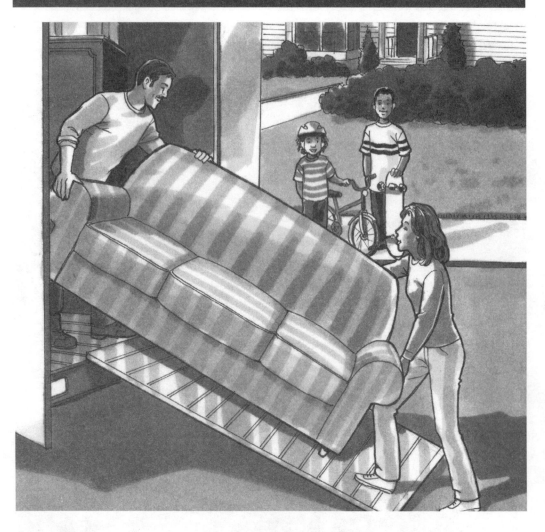

The workers move the sofa. Julie and Paul watch. Who will the new people be? Maybe there will be children.

Which sentence tells a fact?

(A) Julie and Paul do not know the new neighbors.

(B) It will be nice if children move in next door.

Ling hits a home run. His team is happy. They have won the game. They are the champs!

Which sentence tells an opinion?

(A) Ling is a super baseball player.

(B) Ling helped his team win the game.

Mario and his dad walk by each day. They look to see what is being done. They watch the big machines at work. They like to see new buildings rise.

Which sentence tells a fact?

(A) Construction work is hard.

(B) The workers need a crane to make tall buildings.

Leah likes to paint. She uses watercolors. Aunt Su likes her art. She hangs her pictures on the wall.

Which sentence tells an opinion?

(A) Leah's art is very good.

(B) Watercolors are a kind of paint.

Write the following words on the board or chart paper and talk about each one:

museum   library   restaurant   park
store   school   home   new building

A. Exercising Your Skill

Do this together orally as a group or a class.

Listen to the following sentences. These are places found in towns and cities. Think about where you might go to find each of these. Use the words on the board to help you.

1. Where would you find a crane?
2. What place would you go to eat a meal?
3. You find things to read at this place.
4. At what three places might you play soccer?
5. Where would you go to see an exhibit about the past?

B. Expanding Your Skill

Think of a time when you were very happy. What did you do? Did you see or visit someone special? Work with a partner to act out what happened to make you feel good.

C. Exploring Language

Listen while the following story is read. Imagine that you are watching the movers. Think of who the new neighbors will be. Will they have children or a dog? Think of what you would see coming out of the moving van. Finish the sentences with your own words. Then tell who the new neighbors are. What is your opinion of the new people?

The moving van stops in front of the house next door. The movers open the back of the van and pull out a _____. The next thing they take to the house is a heavy _____. I was glad to see that the new neighbors had a _____ . Then the movers carried many boxes of _____ out of the van. _____ was the very last thing to be moved. I knew that the new neighbors liked _____.

D. Expressing Yourself

Draw a map of a town. Choose the buildings and parks you want in your town. Draw roads, buildings, and parks. Tell what you like about the places you chose for your town.

Emily read her story. "I screamed when I saw the mirror. It was dark. I did not know it was me. Then I laughed."

Which sentence tells a fact?

(A) Things can look different in the dark.

(B) Emily's story is funny.

Mr. Ray tells the class about bike safety. He talks about the signs. They learn to watch for cars. They cannot wait to ride the course.

Which sentence tells an opinion?

(A) Bike riders must obey the signs.

(B) It is fun to ride on a bike course.

Mila and Jake put up pictures. They like to help. The board shows the students' art. It shows the books they like best too.

Which sentence tells a fact?

(A) The bulletin board will look great.

(B) The bulletin board is about the ocean.

Joe's mom is a judge. When people cannot
agree, she decides. She hits her gavel on
a block of wood. This keeps order in the
courtroom.

Which sentence tells an opinion?

(A) Judges must know the laws.

(B) Judges have a hard job.

It is raining outside. Students play crab ball in the gym. They have to walk like crabs to get to the ball. They have to kick the ball like a crab.

Which sentence tells an opinion?

    (A) Crab ball is a good game on a rainy day.

    (B) Crabs live in the water.

Many students help paint the mural. The tall boy paints the eagle in the sky. The small boy paints the fish in the water. Amy paints the bear.

Which sentence tells a fact?

(A) A mural is a big picture on a wall.

(B) The students are good artists.

Alex's job is to feed Fred. Fred is a guinea pig. He needs food and water. Fred likes carrots best of all.

Which sentence tells a fact?

(A) Fred is a funny name for a guinea pig.

(B) Guinea pigs eat carrots.

Mrs. Rubin asks, "Where does the apple go?"

"The fruit pile!" Ian says. "It is a fruit."

Which sentence tells a fact?

(A) Apples have seeds.

(B) Apple pie is good to eat.

Gina is glad to see her mom and sister. They will get to meet Nick. Nick's dad and Cody are there too. Now Gina can see his dog.

Which sentence tells an opinion?

(A) The two families will meet.

(B) Cody is a cute dog.

Each student has read ten books. Jamal read ten books about cars. He cannot wait to get his prize.

Which sentence tells an opinion?

(A) Books are fun to read.

(B) Jamal wants to be a race car driver.

Recess is a fun time. Some students like to play catch. Others think writing with chalk is fun.

Which sentence tells a fact?

(A) Playing catch is fun.

44

(B) The students are playing outside.

Paco's dad plays his guitar for the class. Some songs are loud and fast. Some are soft and slow. The students like the songs. They clap after each song.

Which sentence tells an opinion?

(A) A guitar is a musical instrument.

(B) Everyone likes guitar songs.

The firefighters tell about their work. They help put out fires. There is danger in their job. They wear special clothes so they do not get hurt.

Which sentence tells a fact?

(A) Firefighters wear fireproof clothes and boots.

(B) Firefighters are brave.

Zoe and Eric make a fire-safety poster. It tells how to prevent fires. They hope it will help save lives.

Which sentence tells an opinion?

    (A) Fire safety is important.

    (B) Playing with matches can cause a fire.

A. Exercising Your Skill

Using two columns, write on the board or chart paper the following: "My Favorite Subject" and "My Favorite Recess Activity." Ask the students to tell what their favorite subject is and what their favorite recess activity is. Keep a tally of the class favorites. Which subject was liked best by most students? Which recess activity was liked best?

B. Expanding Your Skill

Have the students think about a book or movie that they like. Give each student a sheet of drawing paper, and have them draw a picture that shows part of the book or movie. Help them write the title of the book or movie on their drawing. Put these drawings on a bulletin board. Label the board "Our Favorites."

C. Exploring Language

Listen to the following sentences. Have students say "F" if the sentence is a fact or "O" if it is an opinion.

Onions make me cry.

Larry is the best baseball player in the class.

August is the hottest month of the year.

Flowers need water to grow.

D. Expressing Yourself

Do one of these things.

1. Talk with the class about traffic laws when riding a bicycle.

   (1) You must ride on the right side of the road.

   (2) You must wear a helmet while riding a bicycle.

   (3) You must show a hand signal when you want to turn.

2. Have students make up a game for preschoolers to play. Have them describe how to play the game. Help them write down the rules.

My family has a meeting on Fridays. We talk about our week. We talk about chores. We plan things to do. At the end we play a game!

Which sentence tells a fact?

(A) We meet once a week.

(B) It is good to have meetings.

They cleared the snow from their front door. Then the fun began. They are building a snowman.

Which sentence tells an opinion?

(A) It is nice to play after doing a chore.

(B) A snow shovel is used to clear the snow.

Rose and Liz each have a turn to read. Grandpa listens to them. Rose reads a funny part. Everyone laughs.

Which sentence tells a fact?

(A) Rose and Liz are friends.

(B) Everyone likes funny books.

Baby Emy makes music. Mom comes to see what all the noise is. Mom wonders how Emy got all these things out. Did she have help?

Which sentence tells a fact?

(A) Baby Emy cannot reach the jar of spoons.

(B) The music was loud.

Dad is helping Anita build a bookshelf in her bedroom. She learns to hammer. She learns to drive in screws. She learns to make shelves.

Which sentence tells an opinion?

(A) Anita is learning to use a screwdriver.

(B) Learning a new skill is fun.

Two families are on a camping trip. The tents are up. The fire is going. They ate dinner. Now it is time to make a snack!

Which sentence tells an opinion?

(A) Camping is fun.

(B) The fire helps keep the campers warm.

Dave caught a fish. Grandma says, "It is too small to keep." She takes it off the hook and lets it go. It will grow bigger.

Which sentence tells a fact?

(A) Grandma teaches Dave how to fish.

(B) Fish are good to eat.

TJ and his dad walked to the bottom of the falls. They feel the mist from the water. They cannot hear each other talk. TJ did not know that it would be so loud.

Which sentence tells an opinion?

(A) The mist from the falls feels nice.

(B) Waterfalls can be very tall.

Each week they meet. They learn new tunes. They play many songs. They have fun playing music.

Which sentence tells an opinion?

    (A) Their music sounds good.

    (B) They meet at the house with the piano.

They look at old pictures. Grandma points to a picture of Dad when he was little. He wore a hat and boots that were too big. Dad still likes to wear a hat and boots.

Which sentence tells an opinion?

   (A) Cowboys wear cowboy boots and hats.

   (B) It is fun to look at family pictures.

Greg, Dan, and Mom wash the van. Greg sprays water on Mom. Mom jumps. The water is cold.

Which sentence tells a fact?

(A) It is a lot of fun to wash a van.

(B) Mom is getting wet.

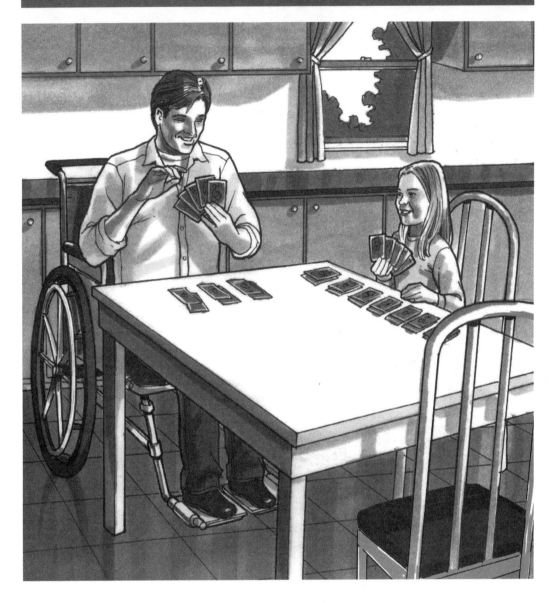

Sally and Dad play cards. There are thirteen sets you can make in this game. Sally has seven sets now. Who will win the game?

Which sentence tells an opinion?

(A) Sally is winning.

(B) Dad likes to play cards.

A. Exercising Your Skill

Write the following sentences on the board or chart paper. Read the sentences to the students one at a time. Have them work with a partner to change the opinion into a fact. Ask for volunteers to share their answers with the class.

1. It is good to see the sunshine again.
2. That new song sounds great.
3. Riding a pony is the most fun you can have.
4. Goldfish are a super pet to have.

B. Expanding Your Skill

Draw the crossword puzzle on the board or chart paper. Work together with the students to complete it.

Clues

1. across   a statement you can prove is true
3. across   facts are statements you can _____
2. down   you can prove facts to be ____

C. Exploring Language

Write the following words on the board:

best prove feel opinion true good fact think

Read the following sentences aloud to the students. Work together as a group to fill in the blanks with (a) word(s) from the list above.

A ___ is a statement you can prove is ___. If you cannot ___ it to be true, it is not a fact. It is an opinion. When the statement is something you ___ or think, it is an ___. When you say "I ___ it is the best," that is your opinion. The words ___ and ___ are used often in opinions.

D. Expressing Yourself

Create several small groups of four or five students. Each group is to pretend their group is a family having a family meeting. Students choose to play the father, mother, and children. Have them hold a family meeting. Volunteers choose a person to talk about their week. Another volunteer talks about their chores. Suggest they plan something fun to do together.